Scary Creatures
SNAKES

Hiss

Written by
Penny Clarke

Illustrated by
Mark Bergin and Carolyn Scrace

Created and designed by
David Salariya

BOOK HOUSE

Author:

Penny Clarke is an author and editor
specialising in information books for children. The
books she has written include titles on natural history,
rainforests and volcanoes, as well as others on
different periods of history. She used to live in central
London, but thanks to modern technology she has
now realised her dream of being able to live and work
in the countryside.

Artists:

Mark Bergin was born in Hastings in 1961.
He studied at Eastbourne College of Art and has
illustrated many children's non-fiction books. He lives
in Bexhill-on-Sea with his wife and three children.

Carolyn Scrace is a graduate of Brighton
College of Art, specialising in design and illustration.
She has worked in animation, advertising and
children's fiction and non-fiction, particularly natural
history.

Series creator:

David Salariya was born in Dundee,
Scotland. In 1989 he established The Salariya Book
Company. He has illustrated a wide range of books
and has created many new series for publishers in the
UK and overseas. He lives in Brighton with his wife,
illustrator Shirley Willis, and their son.

Consultant:

Dr Gerald Legg holds a doctorate in
zoology from Manchester University. He worked in
West Africa for several years as a lecturer and
rainforest researcher. His current position is biologist
at the Booth Museum of Natural History in Brighton.
He is also the author of many natural history books
for children.

Editors:

Stephanie Cole
Karen Barker Smith

Published in Great Britain in 2002 by
Book House, an imprint of
The Salariya Book Company Ltd
25 Marlborough Place, Brighton BN1 1UB

Visit the Salariya Book Company at:
www.salariya.com
www.book-house.co.uk

ISBN 978 1 904194 21 7

A catalogue record for this book is available
from the British Library.

Printed in China.
Printed on paper from sustainable forests.
Reprinted 2007.

Photographic credits:

Anthony Bannister, NHPA: 13, 17, 23, 24
John Foxx Images: 15
Hellio & Van Ingen, NHPA: 10, 16
Daniel Heuclin, NHPA: 11, 14, 20, 25
Karl Switak, NHPA: 26
Martin Wendler, NHPA: 19, 27

Contents

What is a snake? 4

How do snakes move? 6

What's inside a snake? 9

How do snakes see, hear and smell? 10

Why do snakes shed their skin? 12

Do snakes get cold? 14

Are all snakes poisonous? 16

Are snakes strong? 18

Do snakes lay eggs? 20

What do baby snakes look like? 23

Do snakes have enemies? 24

How do snakes swallow eggs? 26

Snakes around the world 28

Snakes facts 30

Glossary 31

Index 32

What is a snake?

Snakes are cold-blooded animals with dry, scaly skins. They breathe with lungs and have backbones. They have no legs. A snake is a type of reptile.

Is a snake a reptile?

Yes, a snake is a reptile.

Is a crocodile a reptile?

Yes, a crocodile is a reptile.

Like snakes and lizards, crocodiles have dry, scaly skins and breathe with lungs. A crocodile's nostrils are high on its head. This means it can breathe and still stay hidden just under the surface of the water.

Most amphibians begin their lives in water and breathe through gills before their lungs grow. They also have a moist, soft skin. Reptiles always breathe with lungs and have scaly skin. A frog is an amphibian, not a reptile.

Is a frog a reptile?

Croak

No, a frog is an amphibian.

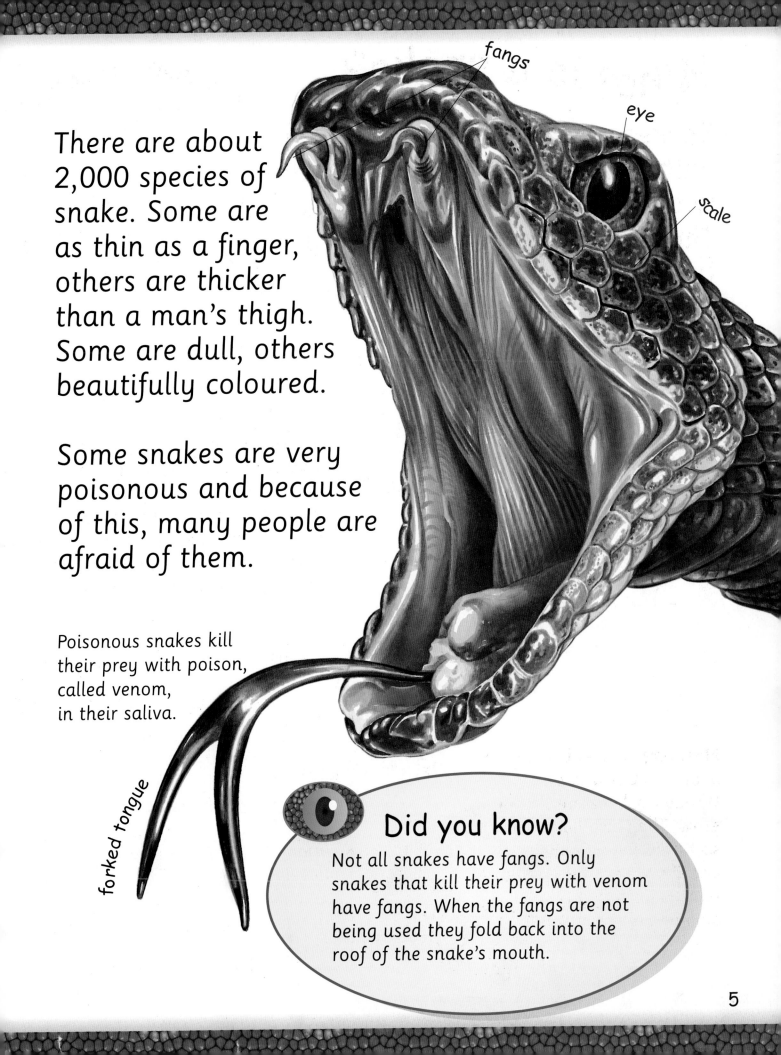

fangs

eye

scale

There are about 2,000 species of snake. Some are as thin as a finger, others are thicker than a man's thigh. Some are dull, others beautifully coloured.

Some snakes are very poisonous and because of this, many people are afraid of them.

Poisonous snakes kill their prey with poison, called venom, in their saliva.

forked tongue

Did you know?

Not all snakes have fangs. Only snakes that kill their prey with venom have fangs. When the fangs are not being used they fold back into the roof of the snake's mouth.

How do snakes move?

Most snakes move in a series of curves. As each curve presses against the ground, it pushes the snake's body forward (diagrams 1 and 2 right).

Some snakes creep along on their stomach scales, pressing their ribs against the ground (diagram 3 right).

Rattlesnakes and vipers use a 'sidewinding' movement to cross loose, hot sand.

Snake movement

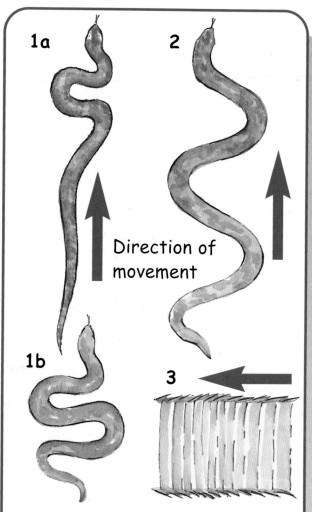

Direction of movement

1a. Front end forms loops, then 1b. the tail is pulled towards the head; 2. Wriggling curves – the outer edge of the loops grip the ground as the snake wriggles forward; 3. Creeping movement – the stomach scales bunch up and push the snake forward like a caterpillar.

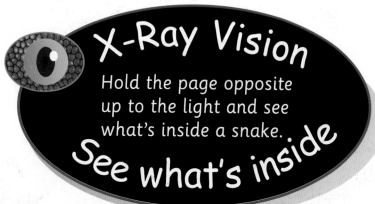

X-Ray Vision

Hold the page opposite up to the light and see what's inside a snake.

See what's inside

overlapping scales

dry skin

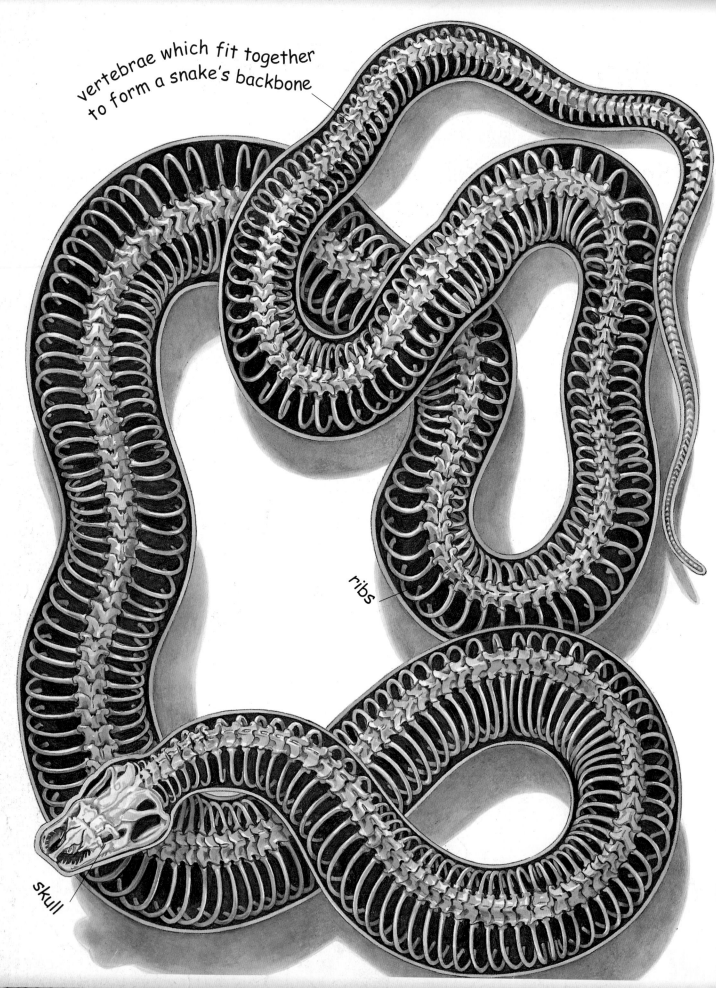

vertebrae which fit together to form a snake's backbone

ribs

skull

What's inside a snake?

Snakes have long, bendy backbones and many ribs. Most snakes have no shoulder, hip or limb bones. Only boas and pythons have two tiny bones to show they once had hind legs.

The ribs protect the organs inside the snake. Organs like the kidneys are long and thin. Many snakes have one lung, not two.

long bendy backbone

teeth

Python skull

This python's skull (left) has sharp, backward curving teeth. Teeth curved like this act as hooks to catch prey and to stop prey escaping if it struggles.

How do snakes see, hear and smell?

Most snakes have good eyesight.

Snakes do not have ears. They 'hear' by feeling vibrations through the ground.

Although they have nostrils, snakes 'smell' with their tongues. These flick in and out of the mouth, picking up scent. The tips of the tongue tuck into a special organ, called Jacobson's organ, in the roof of the mouth. This 'smells' the scent particles.

Cobras (below) are very poisonous. When they sense that they are threatened they defend themselves by 'spitting' venom at their attacker. If it goes in the eye, it can cause blindness.

Cobra

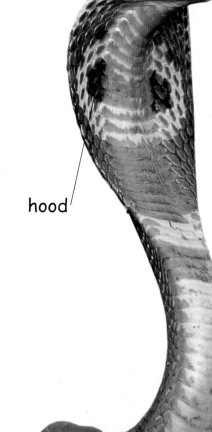

hood

Did you know?

A cobra 'stands up' to attack its prey. Just before it strikes, special ribs swing out to support the 'hood', making it look even more scary.

eye

pit

Pit viper

Pit vipers (above) hunt at night. In front of their eyes are 'pits' that can sense the warmth of the animals that the pit vipers hunt.

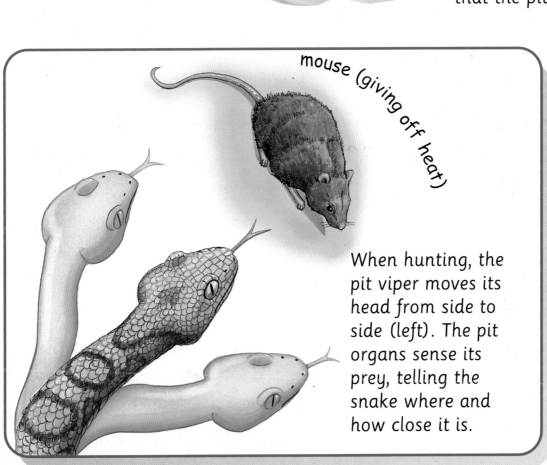

mouse (giving off heat)

When hunting, the pit viper moves its head from side to side (left). The pit organs sense its prey, telling the snake where and how close it is.

How the pit organs work

Why do snakes shed their skin?

Hissss

Snakes cannot grow unless they shed their skins. They have to shed, or moult, the old outer layer regularly.

The snake stretches its jaws or rubs its mouth on something until the old skin splits. As the snake goes on rubbing, the old skin peels off inside-out.

Did you know?

Snakes are covered in hundreds of overlapping scales, with one wide row of scales under the belly. A snake's old skin is so thin that it is almost see-through.

Did you know?

Snakes have no eyelids, so they cannot shut their eyes. Each eye is protected by a tough piece of clear skin called the spectacle.

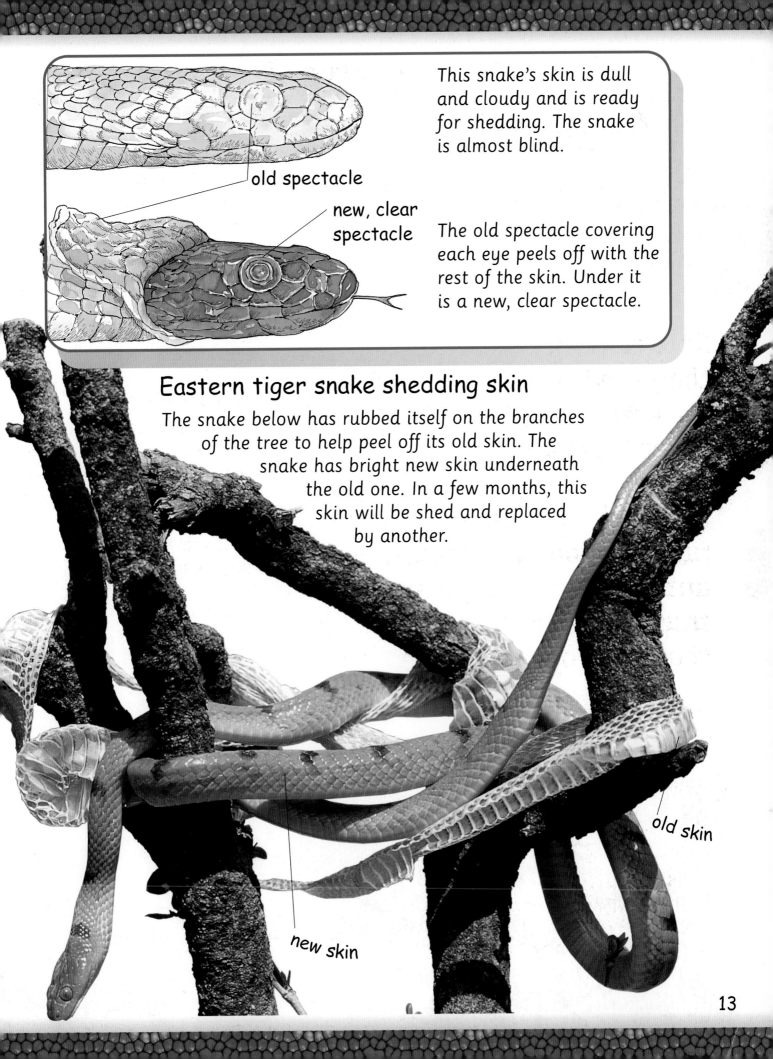

This snake's skin is dull and cloudy and is ready for shedding. The snake is almost blind.

old spectacle

new, clear spectacle

The old spectacle covering each eye peels off with the rest of the skin. Under it is a new, clear spectacle.

Eastern tiger snake shedding skin

The snake below has rubbed itself on the branches of the tree to help peel off its old skin. The snake has bright new skin underneath the old one. In a few months, this skin will be shed and replaced by another.

old skin

new skin

Do snakes get cold?

Snakes are cold-blooded. This means they cannot control the temperature of their bodies. Their temperature depends on the temperature of the air. In winter, when it gets cold outside, snakes go into a sleep-like state called torpor. They cannot keep themselves warm and their bodies cannot work properly in the cold.

Did you know?

At night, when the temperature drops, snakes slow down, just as they do in winter. Next day, as it gets warmer, they wake up again, as they do in spring.

Rattlesnakes in a state of torpor

A puff adder basking in the sun

Did you know?

Snakes like roads and rocky areas. This is because stones and rocks absorb heat from the sun, which makes them warm. Basking on them helps the snakes warm up quickly.

If a warm-blooded animal gets too hot it can sweat or pant to cool itself down. Cold-blooded animals like snakes cannot do this. So snakes living in very hot places spend the hottest part of the day in the shade or burrowed into the ground. If they don't, their body temperature will rise so much they will die.

In spring, the rising temperature warms the snakes and their bodies start working again. They come out of torpor.

Are all snakes poisonous?

Many, but not all, snakes kill by injecting their prey with special poison called venom. Snakes attack with great speed and as their fangs enter their prey's skin, venom is forced into the wound.

This cobra (below) is being 'milked'. Its venom is collected so scientists can make antivenin. Antivenin is medicine that helps people who are bitten by these dangerous snakes.

Fangs are large hollow teeth in the snake's top jaw. Venom from a sac in the jaws runs down the fangs into the prey.

Cobra being milked

Some snakes' venom paralyses the nerves of the prey, some poisons the blood. When the prey cannot struggle any more, the snake swallows it whole.

Snake skull

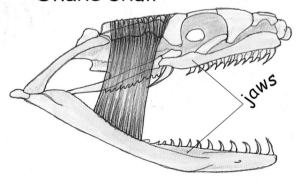

jaws

Spitting cobra

The Mozambique spitting cobra (above) gets its name because it can spit its venom over two metres. It uses strong muscles to force the venom down and out of its fangs in two fine and deadly sprays. This means it can defend itself without getting too close to its attacker.

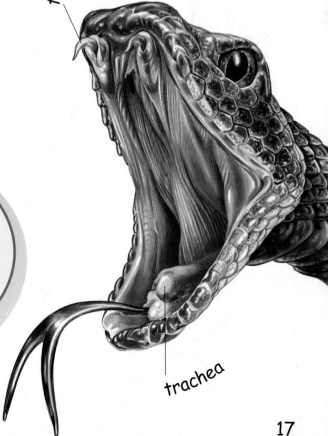

fang

trachea

Did you know?

A snake can push the end of its windpipe (trachea) out of its mouth. If it could not do this, it would choke when it swallowed something very large.

Emerald tree boa

Are snakes strong?

Not all snakes kill with venom. Some crush their prey to death or squeeze them so hard that they cannot breathe. These snakes are called constrictors and they are the largest and most powerful of all snakes. They usually live in trees or by water. They kill by grabbing their prey, looping their muscular bodies around it and then squeezing it hard.

Did you know?

Most snakes have only one lung, but constrictors have two well-developed lungs. Perhaps this is because crushing prey to death uses more energy than attacking it and injecting venom.

Anacondas are snakes that live in South America. They can reach nine metres in length and are extremely strong. They are even able to crush caimans to death (below). Caimans can be over two metres long and are very powerful reptiles.

anaconda

caiman

Anaconda killing a caiman

Do snakes lay eggs?

Yes, many snakes lay eggs. The female lays her eggs in a safe place on the ground. The shells are tough and leathery, not hard like a chicken's egg.

Most female snakes leave their eggs once they have laid them. When they hatch, the young can look after themselves.

eggs

Chinese cobra

Not many snakes look after their eggs, but cobras do. This female Chinese cobra (above) has wrapped herself around her eggs to protect them. They will be quite safe because, like all cobras, she has deadly venom to attack enemies.

X-Ray Vision

Hold the page opposite up to the light and see what's inside a snake's egg.

See what's inside

leathery eggshell

baby snake hatching

amniotic fluid

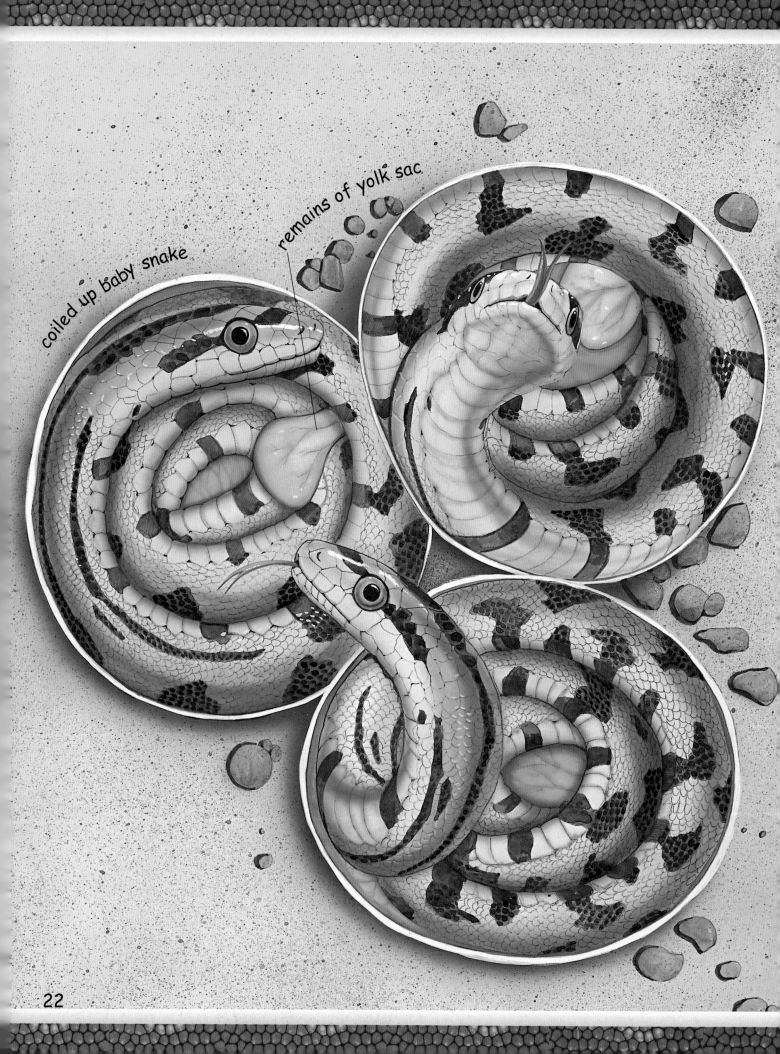

coiled up baby snake

remains of yolk sac

What do baby snakes look like?

Inside each egg is a yolk, which is food for the baby snake.

When the baby snake has eaten all of the yolk, it hatches. It cuts the shell with a special egg tooth and comes out looking like a tiny adult. The egg tooth soon falls out.

Did you know?

Female grass snakes lay up to 40 eggs at a time. They lay them somewhere like a compost heap, because the rotting plants keep the eggs warm and help them hatch quickly.

amniotic fluid

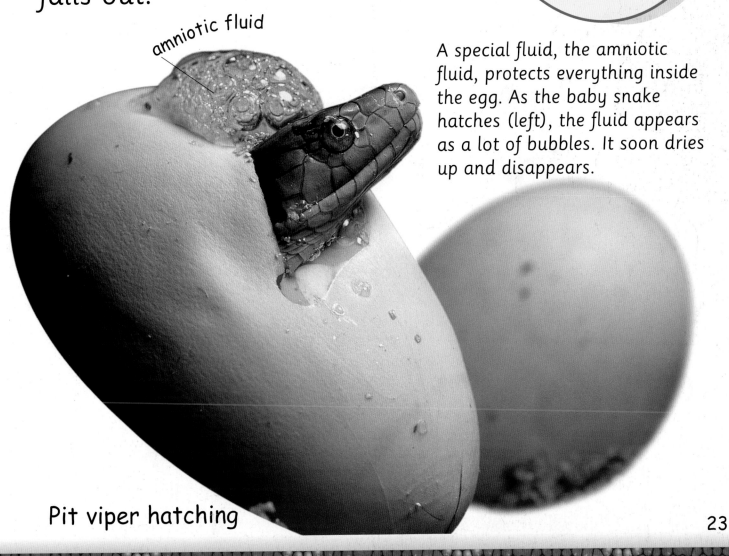

A special fluid, the amniotic fluid, protects everything inside the egg. As the baby snake hatches (left), the fluid appears as a lot of bubbles. It soon dries up and disappears.

Pit viper hatching

Do snakes have enemies?

Even very dangerous snakes have enemies. Snakes defend themselves in different ways. Using venom is one way, but not all snakes are poisonous. Other snakes defend themselves by hiding or escaping quickly. Some snakes look like a more dangerous type of snake.

Did you know?

The red milk snake of North America is harmless. But it has black and yellow bands around its body which make it look like the deadly coral snake. Scientists call it mimicry when a harmless animal has evolved to look like a more dangerous one.

Some snakes protect themselves by pretending to be dead, just as this South African ringneck spitting cobra is doing (right). It lies in an awkward twisted way with its throat showing. When the danger is over it will quickly disappear.

Ringneck spitting cobra

Did you know?

The king cobra, which lives in India, Africa and Southeast Asia, is the world's biggest poisonous snake. It can grow to 5.5 metres and its head can be as big as a human's.

One of India's most dangerous snakes is the cobra, and one of the cobra's greatest enemies is the grey mongoose. The mongoose is able to dodge the cobra's attack very quickly. This makes it a dangerous enemy.

People are snakes' worst enemies. Many species face extinction as they are hunted for their skins. These are used to make items such as the snakeskin boot pictured above.

Cobra attacking mongoose

How do snakes swallow eggs?

Snakes swallow their food whole. They can't chew – their teeth are only used for holding prey or injecting venom.

Here's how the South African egg-eating snake lives up to its name. As it opens its mouth to swallow a chicken's egg, the lower jaw stretches apart.

Many snakes eat prey larger than themselves. They are able to do this because their lower jaws are in two halves, fastened with a ligament which stretches like elastic. The bones which hold the upper jaws to the skull can also move.

Did you know?

All snakes are carnivores. They eat birds, mammals, other snakes, eggs, lizards, frogs, toads and fish. Some of the smaller species eat insects, worms, slugs, snails, ants and termites.

Once the snake has swallowed the egg, wave-like movements of its muscles force it along its body (below). Special 'teeth', which are really parts of the neck vertebrae, slit open the egg and its contents empty into the stomach for digestion. The snake spits out the eggshell, which it does not need. The rest of the egg is digested.

Egg-eating snake after swallowing egg

Snakes around the world

Snakes live in warm areas throughout the world. Because they are cold-blooded, snakes cannot live in polar regions like the Arctic or Antarctic, or in mountainous areas where the temperatures are low.

In the tropics, where it is warm all the time, snakes are active all year round.

The taipan is one of the world's most poisonous snakes. Although it only eats small birds and mammals, its venom sacs hold enough poison to kill up to 80 people.

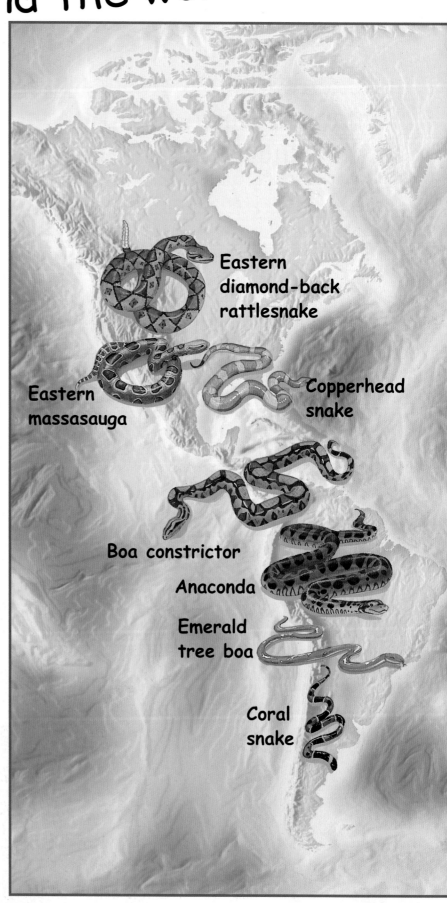

Eastern diamond-back rattlesnake

Eastern massasauga

Copperhead snake

Boa constrictor

Anaconda

Emerald tree boa

Coral snake

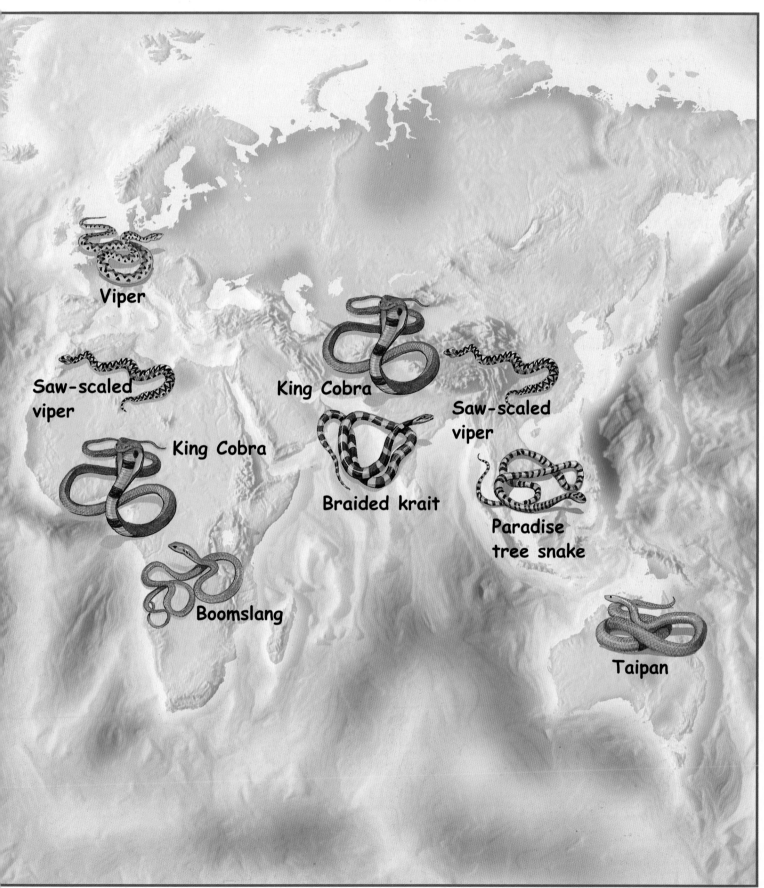

Viper

Saw-scaled
viper

King Cobra

Boomslang

King Cobra

Braided krait

Saw-scaled
viper

Paradise
tree snake

Taipan

 # Snakes facts

The record for the longest snake in the world is held by the reticulated python. A 10 m long one was killed in Indonesia in 1912.

The shortest known snake is the thread snake. It is about 10 cm long and lives in the Caribbean.

The black mamba, found in East Africa, is the world's fastest snake. Over short distances, it can reach speeds of up to 19 kph.

Snakes can live for a long time. In 1977, a boa constrictor at Philadelphia Zoo, in the USA, died aged 40 years. Wild snakes probably do not live as long as this.

The saw-scaled viper bites and kills more people each year than any other snake.

Each year, about 800 people in Sri Lanka die from snake bites.

The speed of a rattlesnake's strike is three metres per second.

A python 5.5 m long has been found with a leopard in its stomach.

Snakes cause roughly 40,000 human deaths every year. About half of these occur in India.

The sea snake is the most poisonous snake on Earth. Its poison is one hundred times more deadly than any other snake's.

Snakes never stop growing, although their growth rate slows down as they get older.

The heaviest snake in the world is the anaconda. It weighs over 270 kg when it is 9 m long.

In some parts of the world, snake-charmers make snakes sway to the music of a flute. The snake can hardly hear the music, though; it may respond to the vibrations of the charmer's tapping foot.

 # Glossary

amphibian A cold-blooded animal that can live in water or on land but breeds in water. A frog is an amphibian.

basking Lying in the warmth of the sun.

cold-blooded An animal whose body temperature changes according to the temperature of the air around it. A snake is cold-blooded.

evolve To develop gradually over thousands or millions of years. Through evolution, animals become better suited to their environment.

extinction When a species of plant or animal no longer exists.

gills Organs with which fish breathe and with which amphibians breathe when they are young.

ligament Strong, flexible and often elastic material connecting two bones.

mimicry When an animal pretends to be another animal.

moult To shed old hair, skin or feathers as new ones grow.

paralyse To make something unable to move or to feel anything.

polar The Earth's coldest regions, north of the Arctic Circle and south of the Antarctic Circle.

prey An animal which is hunted for food by another animal.

reptile A cold-blooded animal that breathes with lungs, such as a snake or a lizard.

species A group of living things that look alike, behave in the same way and can breed with each other.

spectacle A transparent scale that covers a snake's eye to protect it.

torpor A sluggish state that cold-blooded animals go into when the temperature drops.

trachea Another word for the windpipe, the tube in the throat through which animals breathe.

tropics The warmest parts of the Earth.

venom A poison produced by some types of snake.

vertebrae The bones that make up the backbone.

vibrations Very small movements that can sometimes be felt through the ground.

warm-blooded An animal whose temperature remains almost the same, whatever the temperature around it.

Index

A

amniotic fluid 23
amphibians 4, 31
anaconda 19, 30
antivenin 16

B

backbone 4, 9
basking 15, 31
black mamba 30
boas 9
  emerald tree boa 18, 28
boomslang 29
braided krait 29

C

caimans 19
cobras 10, 16, 25
  Chinese cobra 20
  king cobra 25
  Mozambique spitting cobra 17
  ringneck spitting cobra 24
colouring 5
constrictors 18, 28, 30
  boa constrictor 28
copperhead snake 28
coral snake 24, 28
crocodiles 4

D

digestion 27

E

ears 10
Eastern massasauga 28
Eastern tiger snake 13
egg-eating snake 26, 27
eggs 20-21, 22-23
evolution 31
extinction 25, 31

eyesight 10

F

fangs 5, 16, 17
frogs 4, 31

G

gills 4, 31
grass snake 23

H

hunting 11

J

Jacobson's organ 10
jaws 16, 26, 27

K

kidneys 9

L

lizards 4, 31
lungs 4, 9, 18

M

milking 16
mimicry 24, 31
mongoose 25
movement 6
muscles 6, 17, 27

P

paradise tree snake 29
pit organs 11
polar regions 28, 31
prey 5, 10, 11, 16, 18, 26, 27, 31
puff adder 15
pythons 9, 30

R

rattlesnakes 6, 14, 28, 30
red milk snake 24
reptiles 4, 19, 31
ribs 9, 10

S

scales 12, 31
sea snake 30
senses 10-11
skin 4, 12-13, 25, 31
skull 9, 16, 27
snake charmers 30
spectacle 12, 13, 31
spring 14, 15
stomach 27, 30
swallowing 26-27

T

taipan 28, 29
teeth 9, 16, 26
temperature 14-15, 31
thread snake 30
tongues 5, 10
torpor 14, 15, 31
trachea 17, 31

V

venom 5, 10, 16, 17, 18, 20, 24, 26, 28, 31
vertebrae 8, 27, 31
vipers 6, 11, 23, 29

W

winter 14

Y

yolk 23